Bread Ma
Cookbook That You
Will Find Helpful

Bread Machine Recipes for Everyone

BY: Allie Allen

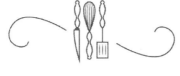

COOK & ENJOY

Copyright 2019 Allie Allen

Copyright Notes

This book is written as an informational tool. While the author has taken every precaution to ensure the accuracy of the information provided therein, the reader is warned that they assume all risk when following the content. The author will not be held responsible for any damages that may occur as a result of the readers' actions.

The author does not give permission to reproduce this book in any form, including but not limited to: print, social media posts, electronic copies or photocopies, unless permission is expressly given in writing.

My Gift to You for Buying My Book!

I would like to extend an exclusive offer to receive free and discounted eBooks every day! This special gift is my way of saying thanks. If you fill in the subscription box below you will begin to receive special offers directly to your email.

Not only that! You will also receive notifications letting you know when an offer will expire. You will never miss a chance to get a free book! Who wouldn't want that?

Fill in the subscriber information below and get started today!

https://allie-allen.getresponsepages.com/

Table of Contents

Easy and Delicious Bread Machine Recipes

SSSSSSSSSSSSSSSSSSSSSSSSSSSSSSSSSSSSSSSSSSSSSSSSSSSS

Chapter 1 - Easy Bread Recipes

SSSSSSSSSSSSSSSSSSSSSSSSSSSSSSSSSSSSSSSSSSSSSSSSSSSSSS

1) Classic Rye Style Bread

This is one bread recipe that I highly recommend preparing, especially if you are looking to switch it up in the kitchen every now and then. This bread is mildly flavored, has a slight sweet taste to it and makes for a nearly perfect sandwich bread. The best type of sandwich to prepare while using this bread is something with corned beef thrown in there.

Serving Size: 1 Loaf

Cooking Time: 1 Hour and 30 Minutes

List of Ingredients:

- 1 Cup of Water, Warm
- 1 ½ teaspoons of Salt
- 1 ½ Tablespoons of Butter, Softened
- 1 tablespoon of Brown Sugar, Light
- ¾ Cup of Rye Flour, Soft
- 2 ¼ Cups of Bread Flour, White and Strong
- 1 ½ teaspoons of Yeast, Fast Acting and Easy Blend Variety

ss

Methods:

1. Fix your mixing bowl securely to your bread maker before you add in any of the ingredients. Make sure that the paddle is also fixed in place securely. Leave your machine unplugged.

2. Mix all three of your flours together until they are thoroughly combine and add this to your machine. Then add in your water and half of your flour mixture into your machine.

3. Then add in your salt, brown sugar, softened butter and your remaining flour into your bread machine next.

4. Make a small well in the top of the flour and carefully place your yeast right into the center of it, making sure that it does not come into contact with any your liquid.

5. Close the lid of your machine and plug it into the wall. Set your machine to the whole-wheat or multigrain bread loaf setting, which you can find in your machines manual. Feel free to alter the crust setting to your liking.

7. Once your bread is fully cooked carefully remove the bowl from your machine and remove the loaf. Place your loaf onto a wire rack to cool.

8. Once your loaf is completely cool remove the paddle of your machine. For the very best results slice up your loaf with a serrated bread knife and serve while it is still warm.

2) Sweet Maple Bread Loaf

Who isn't a fan of sweet breads? With this recipe you can enjoy the sweet and savory taste of maple syrup with every bite of this bread. This is a great bread recipe to prepare to go alongside a large and filling Sunday breakfast or can be served alone with just fresh jam and a bowl of fruit. Either way, it will leave you craving for more.

Serving Size: 1 Loaf

Cooking Time: 45 Minutes

List of Ingredients:

- 1 ½ teaspoons of Yeast, Fast Acting and Easy Blend Variety
- 1 ¼ Cups of Water, Warm
- 1/3 teaspoons of Salt
- ½ Cup of Bread Flour, White and Strong
- 2 ½ Cups of Flour, Whole Wheat
- 2 Tablespoons of Olive Oil, Light
- 4 Tablespoons of Maple Syrup, Your Favorite Brand

sssssssssssssssssssssssssssssssssssssssssssssssssssss

Methods:

1. Fix your mixing bowl securely to your bread maker before you add in any of the ingredients. Make sure that the paddle is also fixed in place securely. Leave your machine unplugged.

2. Mix both of your flours together until they are thoroughly combine and add this to your machine. Then add in your water, oil and maple syrup into your machine next.

3. Then add in your salt and your remaining flour.

4. Make a small well in the top of the flour and carefully place your yeast right into the center of it, making sure that it does not come into contact with any your liquid.

5. Close the lid of your machine and plug it into the wall. Set your machine to the basic white bread loaf setting, which you can find in your machines manual. Feel free to alter the crust setting to your liking.

6. Once your bread is fully cooked carefully remove the bowl from your machine and remove the loaf. Place your loaf onto a wire rack to cool.

7. Once your loaf is completely cool remove the paddle of your machine. For the very best results slice up your loaf with a serrated bread knife and serve while it is still warm.

3) Special Flour Loaf

Specialty breads are now becoming popular nowadays. You can find them virtually anywhere such as your local bakery and your local supermarket. To makes this loaves you need to use a variety of different bread flours and these flours are easily accessible as well. For this particular recipe you will need to use spelt flour. This type of flour will give your loaf a light and fluffy texture and a rich nutty taste that you are going to be craving over and over again.

Serving Size: 1 Loaf

Cooking Time: 1 Hour and 5 Minutes

List of Ingredients:

- 1 ½ Cups of Flour, Spelt
- 1 ½ Cups of Bread Flour, White and Strong
- 1 ¼ Cups of Water, Warm
- 2 Tablespoons of Olive Oil, Light
- 2 teaspoons of Salt
- 2 teaspoons of Sugar, White
- 1 tablespoon of Milk Powder, Dried and Skimmed

- 1 ¼ teaspoons of Yeast, Fast Acting and Easy Blend Variety

ssssssssssssssssssssssssssssssssssssssssssssssssssss

Methods:

1. Fix your mixing bowl securely to your bread maker before you add in any of the ingredients. Make sure that the paddle is also fixed in place securely. Leave your machine unplugged.

2. Mix both of your flours together until they are evenly combined, then add half of this mixture to your machine along with your water and olive oil.

3. Then add in your sugar, milk powder, remaining flour and salt to your mixture and stir to combine.

4. Make a small well in the top of the flour and carefully place your yeast right into the center of it, making sure that it does not come into contact with any your liquid.

5. Close the lid of your machine and plug it into the wall. Set your machine to the basic white loaf setting which you can find in your machines manual. Feel free to alter the crust setting to your liking.

6. Once your bread is fully cooked carefully remove the bowl from your machine and remove the loaf. Place your loaf onto a wire rack to cool.

7. Once your loaf is completely cool remove the paddle of your machine. For the very best results slice up your loaf with a serrated bread knife and serve while it is still warm.

4) Classic Amish White Bread

I there is one thing that Amish know how to do, it is baking bread. Now with this recipe you can enjoy this traditional bread that will leave you craving for more. It is relatively simple to make and goes great with paired along with any food dish regardless if it is for breakfast, lunch, dinner or a simple snack to enjoy. You are going to love this recipe!

Serving Size: 1 Loaf

Cooking Time: 1 Hour and 30 Minutes

List of Ingredients:

- 1 Egg, Large in Size
- 1 teaspoon of Yeast, Fast Acting and Easy Blend Variety
- 1/3 Cup of Sugar, White
- ½ teaspoons of Salt
- ¼ Cup of Canola Oil
- 18 Tablespoons of Water, Warm
- 2 ¾ Cups of Flour, Whole Wheat

sssssssssssssssssssssssssssssssssssssssssssssssssssssss

Methods:

1. Fix your mixing bowl securely to your bread maker before you add in any of the ingredients. Make sure that the paddle is also fixed in place securely. Leave your machine unplugged.

2. First add in your water, oil and half of your flour into your machine

3. Then add in your salt, sugar, large egg and your remaining flour into your machine.

4. Make a small well in the top of the flour and carefully place your yeast right into the center of it, making sure that it does not come into contact with any your liquid.

5. Close the lid of your machine and plug it into the wall. Set your machine to the whole wheat or multigrain bread loaf setting, which you can find in your machines manual. Feel free to alter the crust setting to your liking.

6. Once your bread is fully cooked carefully remove the bowl from your machine and remove the loaf. Place your loaf onto a wire rack to cool.

7. Once your loaf is completely cool remove the paddle of your machine. For the very best results slice up your loaf with a serrated bread knife and serve while it is still warm.

5) Simple White Loaf Bread

This simple yet basic loaf of bread is the perfect bread to start with especially if you are a newcomer to the world of bread making. It is extremely versatile and be adapted to be loaded with a variety of a different toppings. However, this loaf is perfect as is whether you want to lightly toast it and slather it with some butter or whether you just want to serve a few slices along with a cup of tea.

Serving Size: 1 Loaf

Cooking Time: 1 Hour and 20 seconds

List of Ingredients:

- 1 ¼ Cups of Water, Warm
- 2 Tablespoons of Olive Oil, Light
- 3 Cups of Flour, White Bread and Strong
- 1 ¼ teaspoons of Salt
- 1 ¼ teaspoons of Sugar
- 2 Tablespoons of Milk Powder, Dried and Skimmed
- 1 ½ teaspoons of Yeast, Fast Acting and Easy Blend

sssssssssssssssssssssssssssssssssssssssssssssssssssssss

Methods:

1. Fix your mixing bowl securely to your bread maker before adding any of the ingredients. Make sure that the paddle is also secured in place and leave your machine unplugged as you do this

2. Add your water and olive oil to your machine next soon followed by half of your flour.

3. Next add in your salt, sugar, milk powder and remaining flour.

4. Make a well in the top of your flour and carefully place your yeast into it. Make sure that it does not come in to contact with any of the liquid in your mixture.

5. Close the lid of your machine and plug it in. Set the machine to the basic white loaf setting. Your machine's instruction manual will show you how to do it. Feel free to alter the crust setting to your own particular liking.

6. Once cooked carefully remove the bowl from the machine and remove your freshly made loaf and place it onto a wire rack to cool completely.

7. Remove the paddle of your machine and for the best results slice your bread with a serrated knife. Enjoy when you are ready.

6) Asiago Flavored Rosemary Bread Loaf

This bread recipe contains a thick crust yet is very airy on the inside. With the perfect combination of rosemary and asiago cheese, this bread is certainly one that will be giving you that extra kick you have been looking for. While this dough is relatively easy to make, be prepared to have enough dough to make several doughs at once.

Serving Size: 1 Loaf

Cooking Time: 1 Hour and 10 Minutes

List of Ingredients:

- 3 Cups of Flour, All Purpose
- 1 ½ teaspoons of Sea Salt
- 1 ½ teaspoons of Yeast, Fast Acting and Easy Blend Variety
- 1 Cup of Asiago Cheese, Cut into Small Cubes
- 2 Tablespoons of Rosemary, Fresh
- 1 ½ Cups of Water, Warm
- ½ Tablespoons of Olive Oil, Extra Virgin

ss

Methods:

1. Fix your mixing bowl securely to your bread maker before you add in any of the ingredients. Make sure that the paddle is also fixed in place securely. Leave your machine unplugged.

2. First add in your water and half of your flour into your machine.

3. Then follow up by adding in your salt, asiago cheese slices, fresh rosemary and your remaining flour into your bread machine next.

4. Make a small well in the top of the flour and carefully place your yeast right into the center of it, making sure that it does not come into contact with any your liquid.

5. Close the lid of your machine and plug it into the wall. Set your machine to the basic white bread loaf setting, which you can find in your machines manual. Feel free to alter the crust setting to your liking.

7. Once your bread is fully cooked carefully remove the bowl from your machine and remove the loaf. Place your loaf onto a wire rack to cool.

8. Once your loaf is completely cool remove the paddle of your machine. For the very best results slice up your loaf with a serrated bread knife and serve while it is still warm.

7) Everyday Brown Loaf

This is one of the most popular bread loafs that are served in many households today and it is one that is often served in my own home. This bread is great to use to make tasty sandwiches or to serve alone with some fresh jam and melted butter. This is also one of the loaves that can be served alongside virtually any fancy dinner such as smoked salmon or tasty soup recipes.

Serving Size: 1 Loaf

Cooking Time: 1 Hour

List of Ingredients:

- 1 3/8 Cups of Water, Warm
- 1 ½ Tablespoons of Olive Oil, Light
- 3 Cups of Bread Flour, Brown and Whole meal
- 1 ¼ teaspoons of Salt
- 1 tablespoon of Brown Sugar, Soft and Light
- 1 ½ Tablespoons of Milk Powder, Dried and Skimmed
- 2 teaspoons of Yeast, Fast Acting and Easy Blend

ss

Methods:

1. Fix your mixing bowl securely to your bread maker before you add in any of the ingredients. Make sure that the paddle is also fixed in place securely. Leave your machine unplugged.

2. Add in your water and olive oil to your machine followed by half of bread flour.

3. Then add in your remaining dry ingredients and your remaining flour.

4. Make a small well in the top of the flour and carefully place your yeast right into the center of it, making sure that it does not come into contact with any your liquid.

5. Close the lid of your machine and plug it into the wall. Set your machine to the whole meal or whole-wheat setting, which you can find in your machines manual. Feel free to alter the crust setting to your liking.

6. Once your bread is fully cooked carefully remove the bowl from your machine and remove the loaf. Place your loaf onto a wire rack to cool.

7. Once your loaf is completely cool remove the paddle of your machine. For the very best results slice up your loaf with a serrated bread knife and serve while it is still warm.

8) Honey Style Whole Wheat Bread

This is one of the best bread recipes to prepare if you plan on making any sandwiches any time soon. Not only is this bread incredibly delicious, but it is also incredibly healthy for you too. The moment it finished baking, slice it up and make your sandwich to yield the tastiest results.

Serving Size: 1 Loaf

Cooking Time: 1 Hour

List of Ingredients:

- 1 Cup of Water, Warm
- 1 ½ teaspoons of Salt
- 2 Tablespoons of Butter, Softened and Sliced Into Small Pieces
- 2 Tablespoons of Honey, Raw
- 1 ½ Tablespoons of Milk, Powdered and Skimmed
- 1 ½ Cups of Flour, Whole-wheat
- 1 ½ Cups of Bread Flour, White and Strong

- 1 ½ teaspoons of Yeast, Fast Acting and Easy Blend Variety

ssssssssssssssssssssssssssssssssssssssssssssssssssssss

Methods:

1. Fix your mixing bowl securely to your bread maker before you add in any of the ingredients. Make sure that the paddle is also fixed in place securely. Leave your machine unplugged.

2. Mix both of your flours together until they are thoroughly combine and add this to your machine. Then add in your water and half of your flour into your bread machine.

3. Then add in your salt, honey, milk powder and your remaining flour into your bread machine next.

4. Make a small well in the top of the flour and carefully place your yeast right into the center of it, making sure that it does not come into contact with any your liquid.

5. Close the lid of your machine and plug it into the wall. Set your machine to the basic whole-wheat or multigrain bread loaf setting, which you can find in your machines manual. Feel free to alter the crust setting to your liking.

6. Once your bread is fully cooked carefully remove the bowl from your machine and remove the loaf. Place your loaf onto a wire rack to cool.

7. Once your loaf is completely cool remove the paddle of your machine. For the very best results slice up your loaf with a serrated bread knife and serve while it is still warm.

9) Creamy Milk Loaf

No, this loaf is not watery as the name may imply. Instead of being mushy and filled with liquid, this is one loaf of bread that you will want to make over and over again. Adding milk to your loaf of bread makes it much softer, as long as you use the milk while it is at room temperature. Just a word of caution: you may have to make 2 loaves as this bread won't be around for too long in your home.

Serving Size: 1 Loaf

Cooking Time: 1 Hour and 10 Minutes

List of Ingredients:

- 7/8 Cup of Milk, Whole and At Room Temperature
- 3/8 Cup of Water, Warm
- 3 Cups of Bread Flour, White
- 1 ½ teaspoons of Salt
- 2 teaspoons of Sugar, White
- 2 Tablespoons of Butter, Softened
- 1 teaspoon of Yeast, Fast Acting and Easy Blend Variety

SSS

Methods:

1. Fix your mixing bowl securely to your bread maker before adding any of the ingredients. Make sure that the paddle is also secured in place and leave your machine unplugged as you do this

2. Next add in your salt, sugar, soft butter and remaining flour.

3. Make a well in the top of your flour and carefully place your yeast into it. Make sure that it does not come in to contact with any of the liquid in your mixture.

4. Close the lid of your machine and plug it in. Set the machine to the basic white loaf setting. Your machine's instruction manual will show you how to do it. Feel free to alter the crust setting to your own particular liking.

5. Once cooked carefully remove the bowl from the machine and remove your freshly made loaf and place it onto a wire rack to cool completely.

6. Remove the paddle of your machine and for the best results slice your bread with a serrated knife. Enjoy when you are ready.

10) Tasty Strawberry Flavored Bread

Who isn't a fan of strawberries? If you are a strawberry fanatic like I am then you are going to love this recipe. This bread is packed full of sweet tasting strawberry flavor with each and every bite that you take, making it one bread recipe that you are going to be craving over and over again.

Serving Size: 1 Loaf

Cooking Time: 1 Hour and 15 Minutes

List of Ingredients:

- 1 ½ Cups of Flour, All Purpose
- 1 Cup of Sugar, White
- 1 teaspoon of Baking Soda
- ½ Cup of Pecans, Finely Chopped
- ½ Cup of Vegetable Oil
- ½ teaspoons of Baking Powder
- ½ teaspoons of Cinnamon, Ground
- 10 Ounces of Frozen Strawberries, Thawed
- 2 Eggs, Large in Size and Free Range

ss

Methods:

1. Fix your mixing bowl securely to your bread maker before you add in any of the ingredients. Make sure that the paddle is also fixed in place securely. Leave your machine unplugged.

2. Add in your water, oil and half of your all-purpose flour into your bread machine first.

3. Then add in your sugar, cinnamon, baking soda, thawed strawberries, baking powder and your remaining flour into your bread machine.

4. Close the lid of your machine and plug it into the wall. Set your machine to the basic multigrain or wholegrain loaf setting, which you can find in your machines manual. Feel free to alter the crust setting to your liking.

5. Then add in your finely chopped pecans to your machine next the moment that it completes its first kneading cycle.

6. Once your bread is fully cooked carefully remove the bowl from your machine and remove the loaf. Place your loaf onto a wire rack to cool.

7. Once your loaf is completely cool remove the paddle of your machine. For the very best results slice up your loaf with a serrated bread knife and serve while it is still warm.

11) Decadent Chocolate Bread

If you are looking for a bread recipe that can be used as a tasty after dinner dessert, then this is the recipe you have been looking for. Packed full of rich chocolate and sweet to the taste, this is one recipe that is going to leave you craving for more.

Serving Size: 1 Loaf

Cooking Time: 1 Hour and 40 Minutes

List of Ingredients:

- 1 Egg, Large in Size
- 1 teaspoon of Salt
- 1 Cup of Cheese, Cheddar and Shredded
- 1 Cup of Chocolate, Your Favorite Brand and Melted
- 2 teaspoons of Yeast, Fast Acting and Easy Blend Variety
- 2 Cups of Milk, Whole
- 5 Tablespoons of Cocoa Powder
- 2 ½ Cups of Flour, White and Strong
- 8 teaspoons of Sugar, White

sss

Methods:

1. Fix your mixing bowl securely to your bread maker before you add in any of the ingredients. Make sure that the paddle is also fixed in place securely. Leave your machine unplugged.

2. Then add in your milk, egg, cheese and half of your flour into your bread machine.

3. Next add in your salt, sugar, cocoa powder, melted chocolate and your remaining flour into your bread machine.

4. Make a small well in the top of the flour and carefully place your yeast right into the center of it, making sure that it does not come into contact with any your liquid.

5. Close the lid of your machine and plug it into the wall. Set your machine to the basic white bread loaf setting, which you can find in your machines manual. Feel free to alter the crust setting to your liking.

6. Once your bread is fully cooked carefully remove the bowl from your machine and remove the loaf. Place your loaf onto a wire rack to cool.

7. Once your loaf is completely cool remove the paddle of your machine. For the very best results slice up your loaf with a serrated bread knife and serve while it is still warm.

12) European Style Dark Bread

This is one loose interpretation of a Russian Bread Loaf. While there are certainly more ingredients in this recipe that any of the previous recipes, I promise that the end result will be well worth the time you will spend preparing it. I recommend serving this bread along with a tasty smoked salmon dinner or with a filling and savory stewed dinner.

Serving Size: 1 Loaf

Cooking Time: 1 Hour and 5 Minutes

List of Ingredients:

- 3/5 Cup of Bread Flour, Whole meal, Brown and Strong
- 1 Cup of Rye Flour
- 1 2/3 Cups of Bread Flour, White and Strong
- 1 5/8 Cup of Water
- 2 Tablespoons of Olive Oil, Light
- 2 ½ Tablespoons of Molasses
- 2/5 Cup of Oat Bran
- ¾ Cup of Breadcrumbs, Dried
- 1 ½ Tablespoons of Cocoa Powder

- 2 Tablespoons of Instant Coffee
- 1 teaspoon of Caraway Seeds
- ¼ teaspoons of Fennel Seeds
- 1 ½ teaspoons of Salt
- 1 ½ teaspoons of Yeast, Fast Acting and Easy Blend Variety

sssssssssssssssssssssssssssssssssssssssssssssssssssss

Methods:

1. Fix your mixing bowl securely to your bread maker before you add in any of the ingredients. Make sure that the paddle is also fixed in place securely. Leave your machine unplugged.

2. Mix all three of your flours together until they are thoroughly combine and add this to your machine. Then add in your water, oil and molasses.

3. Then add in your oat bran, breadcrumbs, instant coffee and cocoa powder together. Then add I your fennel seeds, caraway seeds, salt and your remaining flour.

4. Make a small well in the top of the flour and carefully place your yeast right into the center of it, making sure that it does not come into contact with any your liquid.

5. Close the lid of your machine and plug it into the wall. Set your machine to the whole meat or whole meal setting, which you can find in your machines manual. Feel free to alter the crust setting to your liking.

6. Then add in your finely chopped walnuts to your machine next the moment that it completes its first kneading cycle.

7. Once your bread is fully cooked carefully remove the bowl from your machine and remove the loaf. Place your loaf onto a wire rack to cool.

8. Once your loaf is completely cool remove the paddle of your machine. For the very best results slice up your loaf with a serrated bread knife and serve while it is still warm.

13) Fast Baking Banana Bread

Banana bread is another holiday bread favorite that you absolutely have to try making for yourself. This is a great recipe to prepare for Thanksgiving as it tastes great when paired alongside a freshly baked turkey. This bread recipe will satisfy even the pickiest of eaters and will leave your guests wanting more of it.

Serving Size: 1 Loaf

Cooking Time: 1 Hour and 20 Minutes

List of Ingredients:

- 1 teaspoon of Baking Powder
- ½ teaspoons of Baking Soda
- 2 Bananas, Peeled and Sliced into Halves
- 2 Cups of Flour, All Purpose
- 2 Eggs, Large in Size
- 3 Tablespoons of Vegetable Oil
- ¾ Cup of Sugar, White

ssssssssssssssssssssssssssssssssssssssssssssssssssssss

Methods:

1. Fix your mixing bowl securely to your bread maker before you add in any of the ingredients. Make sure that the paddle is also fixed in place securely. Leave your machine unplugged.

2. First add in your vegetable oil, eggs and half of your flour into your machine.

3. Then add in your sugar, baking powder, baking soda, peeled banana halves and your remaining flour into your machine next.

4. Make a small well in the top of the flour and carefully place your yeast right into the center of it, making sure that it does not come into contact with any your liquid.

5. Close the lid of your machine and plug it into the wall. Set your machine to the basic white bread loaf setting, which you can find in your machines manual. Feel free to alter the crust setting to your liking.

6. Once your bread is fully cooked carefully remove the bowl from your machine and remove the loaf. Place your loaf onto a wire rack to cool.

7. Once your loaf is completely cool remove the paddle of your machine. For the very best results slice up your loaf with a serrated bread knife and serve while it is still warm.

14) Everyday White and Egg Loaf

Many people do not know that when you add egg to your bread dough, it will give the bread a much richer flavor making it the best loaf to make for an early morning breakfast. Serve this loaf alongside a side of bacon and tomatoes to make a filling and healthy breakfast meal. This is one loaf of bread that you are going to want to make as often as possible regardless of what time of the day it is.

Serving Size: 1 Loaf

Cooking Time: 1 Hour and 30 Minutes

List of Ingredients:

- 1 Egg Plus 1 Egg Yolk, Free Range and Large In Size
- 3 2/5 Cup of Bread Flour, White and Strong
- 1 3/8 Cup of Water, Warm
- 1 ½ teaspoons of Salt
- 2 teaspoons of Sugar, White
- 2 Tablespoons of Butter, Softened
- 1 teaspoon of Yeast, Fast Acting and Easy Blend

sss

Methods:

1. Fix your mixing bowl securely to your bread maker before adding any of the ingredients. Make sure that the paddle is also secured in place and leave your machine unplugged as you do this.

2. Next using a medium sized mixing bowl add in your whole egg and egg yolk with your water and whisk together until thoroughly beaten. Add this mixture to your bread machine along with half of your bread flour.

3. Next add in your salt, sugar, softened butter and remaining flour.

4. Make a well in the top of your flour and carefully place your yeast into it. Make sure that it does not come in to contact with any of the liquid in your mixture.

5. Close the lid of your machine and plug it in. Set the machine to the basic white loaf setting. Your machine's instruction manual will show you how to do it. Feel free to alter the crust setting to your own particular liking.

6. Once cooked carefully remove the bowl from the machine and remove your freshly made loaf and place it onto a wire rack to cool completely.

7. Remove the paddle of your machine and for the best results slice your bread with a serrated knife. Enjoy when you are ready.

15) Classic Portuguese Bread

This classic bread recipe will taste as if you are sitting in a tiny café right in the middle of Portugal. It is sweet to the taste so you can rest assured that it will satisfy your sweet tooth. This is one of the most perfect bread recipes to prepare during the holiday season because it will get even the grumpiest of Grinch's to get into the holiday spirit.

Serving Size: 1 Loaf

Cooking Time: 1 Hour and 40 Minutes

List of Ingredients:

- 1 Cup of Milk, Whole
- 1 Egg, Large in Size and Beaten
- 1/3 Cup of Sugar, White
- 2 ½ teaspoons of Yeast, Fast Acting and Easy Blend Variety
- 2 Tablespoons of Butter, Softened
- 3 Cups of Bread Flour, White and Strong
- ¾ teaspoons of Salt

sssssssssssssssssssssssssssssssssssssssssssssssssssssss

Methods:

1. Fix your mixing bowl securely to your bread maker before you add in any of the ingredients. Make sure that the paddle is also fixed in place securely. Leave your machine unplugged.

2. The first thing that you will want to do is add in your water, oil and milk into your machine

3. Then add in your salt, sugar, softened butter, beaten egg and your remaining flour.

4. Make a small well in the top of the flour and carefully place your yeast right into the center of it, making sure that it does not come into contact with any your liquid.

5. Close the lid of your machine and plug it into the wall. Set your machine to the basic white bread loaf setting, which you can find in your machines manual. Feel free to alter the crust setting to your liking.

6. Once your bread is fully cooked carefully remove the bowl from your machine and remove the loaf. Place your loaf onto a wire rack to cool.

7. Once your loaf is completely cool remove the paddle of your machine. For the very best results slice up your loaf with a serrated bread knife and serve while it is still warm.

16) Tasty Pistachio Loaf

Adding some extra ingredients to your bread mix is not something that has been done recently. Adding pistachios to this recipe will give your loaf brand new flavors that you haven't been able to taste before. I recommend serving this loaf with a traditional Moroccan or Indian dish to yield the best results. Also don't hesitate to serve this bread with a variety of different cheeses as an appetizer or an easy lunch recipe.

Serving Size: 1 Loaf

Cooking Time: 1 Hour

List of Ingredients:

- ¾ Cup of Pistachios, Shelled
- 1 ¼ Cups of Water, Warm
- 3 Cups of Bread Flour, White and Strong
- 2 Tablespoons of Pistachio Oil or Nut Oil
- 1 ½ teaspoons of Salt
- 2 teaspoons of Sugar, White
- 1 ½ teaspoons of Yeast, Fast Acting and Easy Blend

sss

Methods:

1. The first thing that you will want to do is place your pistachios into a bowl and cover them with some boiling water and leave them for a couple of minutes. Drain and remove the skins. Place the shelled nuts into a bowl covered with water and set aside to use later on.

2. Fix your mixing bowl securely to your bread maker before you add in any of the ingredients. Make sure that the paddle is also fixed in place securely. Leave your machine unplugged.

3. Add in your water and olive oil to your machine followed by half of bread flour.

4. Then add in your white sugar, salt and your remaining flour.

5. Make a small well in the top of the flour and carefully place your yeast right into the center of it, making sure that it does not come into contact with any your liquid.

6. Close the lid of your machine and plug it into the wall. Set your machine to the specialty bread setting, which you can find in your machines manual. Feel free to alter the crust setting to your liking.

7. Next add in your pistachios to your machine was the first kneading cycle is complete.

8. Once your bread is fully cooked carefully remove the bowl from your machine and remove the loaf. Place your loaf onto a wire rack to cool.

9. Once your loaf is completely cool remove the paddle of your machine. For the very best results slice up your loaf with a serrated bread knife and serve while it is still warm.

17) Zesty Parsley Whole Wheat Bread

Parsley is not an ingredient that is used in my bread loaf recipes and that is a shame because it is actually quite tasty. With this bread recipe you will be able to taste the hint of parsley you use but it will not overload the bread with its intense flavor. This bread is a great bread to use to make sandwiches or to cut up and serve alongside a hearty soup.

Serving Size: 1 Loaf

Cooking Time: 1 Hour and 15 Minutes

List of Ingredients:

- 1 ½ Cups of Water, Warm
- 1 ½ teaspoons of Rosemary, Dried
- 1 ½ teaspoons of Thyme, Dried
- 1 ½ teaspoons of Salt
- 1 tablespoon of Parsley, Heaping and Dried
- 2 Cups of Bread Flour, White and Strong
- 2 Cups of Flour, Whole-wheat

- 2 teaspoons of Yeast, Fast Acting and Easy Blend Variety
- 3 Tablespoons of Honey, Raw
- 3 Tablespoons of Olive Oil, Light
- 3 Tablespoons of Milk, Powdered and Skimmed
- 4 teaspoons of Wheat Gluten, Vital

ssssssssssssssssssssssssssssssssssssssssssssssssssss

Methods:

1. Fix your mixing bowl securely to your bread maker before you add in any of the ingredients. Make sure that the paddle is also fixed in place securely. Leave your machine unplugged.

2. Mix both of your flours together until they are thoroughly combine and add this to your machine. Then add in your water, oil and honey to your machine.

3. Then add in your salt, dried herbs, wheat gluten milk powder and your remaining flour.

4. Make a small well in the top of the flour and carefully place your yeast right into the center of it, making sure that it does not come into contact with any your liquid.

5. Close the lid of your machine and plug it into the wall. Set your machine to the basic white bread loaf or whole-wheat loaf setting, which you can find in your machines manual. Feel free to alter the crust setting to your liking.

6. Once your bread is fully cooked carefully remove the bowl from your machine and remove the loaf. Place your loaf onto a wire rack to cool.

7. Once your loaf is completely cool remove the paddle of your machine. For the very best results slice up your loaf with a serrated bread knife and serve while it is still warm.

18) Savory Pine Nut Loaf

This is yet another nutty bread recipe for you to try and it is going to be one that you are going to fall in love with. I recommend making this recipe during the holiday season such as on Christmas and Easter. Just a word of caution: saffron, one of the ingredients that you will be using, can tend to be a bit on the pricey side during the holidays so be braced for that when you get to the supermarket. This is one smooth and soft loaf of bread that you will want to make again and again.

Serving Size: 1 Loaf

Cooking Time: 1 Hour and 20 Minutes

List of Ingredients:

- 3/8 Cup of Pine Nuts
- ½ teaspoons of Saffron, Strands
- 1 ¼ Cups of Water, Warm
- 2 Tablespoons of Olive Oil, Light
- 3 Cups of Bread Flour, White and Strong
- 1 ½ teaspoons of Salt
- 2 teaspoons of Brown Sugar, Light and Soft

- 1 ½ teaspoons of Yeast, Fast Acting and Easy Blend Variety

sssssssssssssssssssssssssssssssssssssssssssssssssssss

Methods:

1. The first thing that you will want to do is to lightly toast your pine nuts over low heat until the nuts turn light brown in color. Set aside for later use.

2. Then place your strands of saffron into a small sized bowl that is covered with at least 1 to 2 tablespoons of boiling water. Stir well and set aside until the water cools completely.

3. While your saffron mix is cooling fix your mixing bowl securely to your bread maker before you add in any of the ingredients. Make sure that the paddle is also fixed in place securely. Leave your machine unplugged.

4. Add in your water, saffron mixture and olive oil to your machine followed by half of bread flour.

5. Then add in your sugar, salt and your remaining flour.

6. Make a small well in the top of the flour and carefully place your yeast right into the center of it, making sure that it does not come into contact with any your liquid.

7. Close the lid of your machine and plug it into the wall. Set your machine to the specialty bread setting, which you can find in your machines manual. Feel free to alter the crust setting to your liking.

8. Then add in your lightly toasted pine nuts into your machine the moment that the first kneading cycle is complete.

9. Once your bread is fully cooked carefully remove the bowl from your machine and remove the loaf. Place your loaf onto a wire rack to cool.

10. Once your loaf is completely cool remove the paddle of your machine. For the very best results slice up your loaf with a serrated bread knife and serve while it is still warm.

19) Healthy Multigrain Bread

If you are looking to add a bit of multigrain to you diet, this is the best bread recipe to do it with. Relatively easy to make and incredibly tasty, this is one bread loaf you are going to want to make over and over again. Serve this with some scrambled or poached eggs in the morning or alongside a filling stew in the afternoon to compliment your meal.

Serving Size: 1 Loaf

Cooking Time: 1 Hour

List of Ingredients:

- 1 ¼ Cups of Water, Warm
- 2 Tablespoons of Butter, Softened
- 1 1/3 Cups of Flour, All Purpose
- 1 1/3 Cups of Flour, Whole Wheat
- 1 Cup of Multigrain Hot Cereal
- 3 Tablespoons of Brown Sugar, packed
- 1 ¼ teaspoons of Salt
- 2 ½ teaspoons of Yeast, Fast Acting and Easy Blend Variety

Methods:

1. Fix your mixing bowl securely to your bread maker before you add in any of the ingredients. Make sure that the paddle is also fixed in place securely. Leave your machine unplugged.

2. Mix both of your flours together until they are thoroughly combine and add this to your machine. Then add in your water and hot cereal to your machine

3. Then add in your salt, brown sugar, soft butter and your remaining flour.

4. Make a small well in the top of the flour and carefully place your yeast right into the center of it, making sure that it does not come into contact with any your liquid.

5. Close the lid of your machine and plug it into the wall. Set your machine to the whole wheat or multigrain loaf setting, which you can find in your machines manual. Feel free to alter the crust setting to your liking.

6. Once your bread is fully cooked carefully remove the bowl from your machine and remove the loaf. Place your loaf onto a wire rack to cool.

7. Once your loaf is completely cool remove the paddle of your machine. For the very best results slice up your loaf with a serrated bread knife and serve while it is still warm.

20) Nutty Style Cranberry Bread Loaf

This is yet another sweet tasting bread recipe that the entire family will enjoy. Sweet to taste and filled with a nutty flavor that you are going to love, this is one bread recipe that you are going to want to enjoy over and over again. Feel free to use whatever nuts you want in this recipe. It is extremely versatile so get as creative with it as you want.

Serving Size: 1 Loaf

Cooking Time: 1 Hour and 15 Minutes

List of Ingredients:

- ¼ Cup of Oats, Rolled
- ¼ Cup of Water, Warm
- 1 Cup of Buttermilk, Room Temperature
- 1 Egg, Large in Size
- 3 Tablespoons of Honey, Raw
- 1 ½ Tablespoons of Butter, Softened
- 3 Cups of Bread Flour, White and Strong
- 1 teaspoon of Salt

- ¼ teaspoons of Baking Soda
- ½ teaspoons of Cinnamon, Ground
- 2 teaspoons of Yeast, Fast Acting and Easy Blend Variety
- ¾ Cup of Cranberries, Dried
- ½ Cup of Walnuts, Finely Chopped

sssssssssssssssssssssssssssssssssssssssssssssssssssss

Methods:

1. Fix your mixing bowl securely to your bread maker before you add in any of the ingredients. Make sure that the paddle is also fixed in place securely. Leave your machine unplugged.

2. First add in your water, oil, rolled oats and half of your flour into your bread machine.

3. Then add in your salt, honey, buttermilk, softened butter, large egg, baking soda, cinnamon and your remaining flour into your bread machine next

4. Make a small well in the top of the flour and carefully place your yeast right into the center of it, making sure that it does not come into contact with any your liquid.

5. Close the lid of your machine and plug it into the wall. Set your machine to the basic white bread loaf setting, which you can find in your machines manual. Feel free to alter the crust setting to your liking.

6. Then add in your finely chopped walnuts and cranberries to your machine next the moment that it completes its first kneading cycle.

7. Once your bread is fully cooked carefully remove the bowl from your machine and remove the loaf. Place your loaf onto a wire rack to cool.

8. Once your loaf is completely cool remove the paddle of your machine. For the very best results slice up your loaf with a serrated bread knife and serve while it is still warm.

21) Healthy Beetroot Bread Loaf

While this loaf of bread may not seem like it would be appetizing, take my word for it when I say it is. Beetroot is one kind of vegetable that is very rarely used in the world and many people underestimate its healthy qualities. This is a perfect recipe to prepare to go alongside a healthy lunch salad or perfect if served alongside a dinner time stew. It will leave you warm and fuzzy, especially during the cold winter months.

Serving Size: 1 Loaf

Cooking Time: 1 Hour and 5 Minutes

List of Ingredients:

- ¾ Cup of Water, Warm
- 1 ½ Cups of Beetroot, Raw and Freshly Grated
- 3 2/5 Cups of Bread Flour, Strong and White
- 2 tablespoons of Butter, Softened
- 2 teaspoons of Salt
- 1 ½ teaspoons of Sugar, White

- 1 ½ teaspoons of Yeast, Fast Acting and Easy Blend Variety
- 2 Spring Onions, Large in Size and Chopped Finely

sssssssssssssssssssssssssssssssssssssssssssssssssssss

Methods:

1. Fix your mixing bowl securely to your bread maker before you add in any of the ingredients. Make sure that the paddle is also fixed in place securely. Leave your machine unplugged.

2. First add in your water and grated beetroot into your machine. Then add in half of your flour.

3. Next add in your salt, sugar, soft butter and your remaining flour.

4. Make a small well in the top of the flour and carefully place your yeast right into the center of it, making sure that it does not come into contact with any your liquid.

5. Close the lid of your machine and plug it into the wall. Set your machine to the basic white bread loaf setting, which you can find in your machines manual. Feel free to alter the crust setting to your liking.

6. Then add in your finely chopped spring onions to your machine next when your machine completes its first kneading cycle.

7. Once your bread is fully cooked carefully remove the bowl from your machine and remove the loaf. Place your loaf onto a wire rack to cool.

8. Once your loaf is completely cool remove the paddle of your machine. For the very best results slice up your loaf with a serrated bread knife and serve while it is still warm.

22) Malted Style Tea Loaf

I do not recommend making this loaf of bread until you have completely mastered most of the recipes listed before this one. This loaf of bread is perfect to serve with an afternoon coffee or tea and can be slathered with some fresh marmalade to make an easy and delicious breakfast meal.

Serving Size: 1 Loaf

Cooking Time: 1 Hour

List of Ingredients:

- 1 ¼ Cups of Water, Warm
- 1 ½ Tablespoons of Syrup, Golden
- 2 Tablespoons of Malt, Extract
- 3 2/5 Cup of Bread Flour, White and Strong
- 1 teaspoon of Salt
- 4 Tablespoons of Butter, Soft
- 2 Tablespoons of Milk Powder, Dried and Skimmed
- 1 teaspoon of Yeast, Fast Acting and Easy Blend Variety
- ½ Cup of Sultanas, Plump

sss

Methods:

1. Fix your mixing bowl securely to your bread maker before you add in any of the ingredients. Make sure that the paddle is also fixed in place securely. Leave your machine unplugged.

2. Add in your water, golden syrup and malt to your machine followed by half of bread flour.

3. Then add in your salt, soft butter, milk powder and your remaining flour.

4. Make a small well in the top of the flour and carefully place your yeast right into the center of it, making sure that it does not come into contact with any your liquid.

5. Close the lid of your machine and plug it into the wall. Set your machine to the basic white loaf setting, which you can find in your machines manual. Feel free to alter the crust setting to your liking.

6. Next add in your sultanas the moment the first kneading cycle is complete.

7. Once your bread is fully cooked carefully remove the bowl from your machine and remove the loaf. Place your loaf onto a wire rack to cool.

8. Once your loaf is completely cool remove the paddle of your machine. For the very best results slice up your loaf with a serrated bread knife and serve while it is still warm.

23) Sweet Tasting Cinnamon and Apple Bread Loaf

While there are many recipes within this book that contain fruit juice, most of them will not be as delicious as this one. This recipe is a perfect one to make in the middle of the fall season as the apple and cinnamon flavors will put you into the fall mood and give you that warmth you have been looking for. Just spread some fresh marmalade or jam on the loaf to make a tasty and fulfilling afternoon snack.

Serving Size: 1 Loaf

Cooking Time: 45 Minutes

List of Ingredients:

- 1 ¼ Cups of Apple Juice, Fresh
- 2 Tablespoons of Olive Oil, Light
- 1 ½ Cups of Bread Flour, White and Strong
- 1 ¼ teaspoons of Salt
- 1 ½ teaspoons of Sugar, White
- 1 tablespoon of Cinnamon, Ground

- 1 ¼ teaspoons of Yeast, Fast Acting and Easy Blend Variety

sssssssssssssssssssssssssssssssssssssssssssssssss

Methods:

1. Fix your mixing bowl securely to your bread maker before you add in any of the ingredients. Make sure that the paddle is also fixed in place securely. Leave your machine unplugged.

2. Next add in your fresh apple juice and olive oil into your machine. Then add in half of your flour.

3. Then add in your salt, sugar, ground cinnamon and your remaining flour into your machine next.

4. Make a small well in the top of the flour and carefully place your yeast right into the center of it, making sure that it does not come into contact with any your liquid.

5. Close the lid of your machine and plug it into the wall. Set your machine to the basic white bread loaf setting, which you can find in your machines manual. Feel free to alter the crust setting to your liking.

6. Once your bread is fully cooked carefully remove the bowl from your machine and remove the loaf. Place your loaf onto a wire rack to cool.

7. Once your loaf is completely cool remove the paddle of your machine. For the very best results slice up your loaf with a serrated bread knife and serve while it is still warm.

24) Filling Potato and Herb Loaf

If you are having trouble getting your children to eat vegetables or potatoes, this is one recipe that you need to try for yourself. It will help to get your children to eat their veggies in a tasty and creative way and will leave you feeling full and satisfied. This loaf of bread is incredibly soft and most, making it the most perfect bread to accompany a plate of scrambled or poaches eggs in the morning.

Serving Size: 1 Loaf

Cooking Time: 1 Hour and 10 Minutes

List of Ingredients:

- 1 Cup of Water, Warm
- 3 Tablespoons of Olive Oil, Light
- 3 25 Cups of Bread Flour, White and Strong
- 1 ½ Cups of Potato, Fully Cooked and Mashed
- 1 ½ teaspoons of Salt
- 2 teaspoons of Sugar, White
- 1 ½ teaspoons of Milk Powder, Dried and Skimmed

- 1 ½ teaspoons of Yeast, Fast Acting and Easy Blend Variety

ssssssssssssssssssssssssssssssssssssssssssssssssssssssss

Methods:

1. The first thing that you will want to do is cut up your potatoes and mash them, making sure to keep at least 1 cup of the water that the potatoes were cooking in. Set the mashed potatoes aside until they cool completely.

2. Fix your mixing bowl securely to your bread maker before you add in any of the ingredients. Make sure that the paddle is also fixed in place securely. Leave your machine unplugged.

3. Add in your water and olive oil to your machine followed by half of bread flour.

4. Then add in your mashed potatoes, sugar, salt milk powder and your remaining flour.

5. Make a small well in the top of the flour and carefully place your yeast right into the center of it, making sure that it does not come into contact with any your liquid.

6. Close the lid of your machine and plug it into the wall. Set your machine to the basic white loaf setting, which you can find in your machines manual. Feel free to alter the crust setting to your liking.

7. Once your bread is fully cooked carefully remove the bowl from your machine and remove the loaf. Place your loaf onto a wire rack to cool.

8. Once your loaf is completely cool remove the paddle of your machine. For the very best results slice up your loaf with a serrated bread knife and serve while it is still warm.

25) Healthy Fig and Rosemary Bread Loaf

When you compare two foods together, there is nothing better than bread and cheese as a tasty snack and the moment you make this loaf you will want to make it over and over again. This bread is extremely versatile and you can easily use this in a variety of different ways. Regardless if you serve this bread for breakfast, lunch or dinner, I promise you that you are going to fall in love with it.

Serving Size: 1 Loaf

Cooking Time: 1 Hour

List of Ingredients:

- 5/8 Cups of Water, Warm
- 4 Tablespoons of Olive Oil, Light
- 2 Eggs, Large in Size and Free Range
- 3 2/5 Cups of Bread Flour, White and Strong
- 1 ½ teaspoons of Salt
- 2 teaspoons of Sugar, White

- 1 ½ Tablespoons of Rosemary, Fresh and Chopped Finely
- 2 Tablespoons of Milk Powder, Dried and Skimmed
- 1 teaspoon of Yeast, Fast Acting and Easy Blend Variety
- 2/3 Cup of Figs, Dried and Finely Chopped

ssssssssssssssssssssssssssssssssssssssssssssssssssss

Methods:

1. Fix your mixing bowl securely to your bread maker before you add in any of the ingredients. Make sure that the paddle is also fixed in place securely. Leave your machine unplugged.

2. Next add in your warm water, eggs and olive oil to your machine. Follow up by adding half of your sugar.

3. Then add in your salt, rosemary, sugar, milk powder and your remaining flour.

4. Make a small well in the top of the flour and carefully place your yeast right into the center of it, making sure that it does not come into contact with any your liquid.

5. Close the lid of your machine and plug it into the wall. Set your machine to the basic white bread loaf setting, which you can find in your machines manual. Feel free to alter the crust setting to your liking.

6. Then add in your finely chopped dried figs to your machine next the moment that it completes its first kneading cycle.

7. Once your bread is fully cooked carefully remove the bowl from your machine and remove the loaf. Place your loaf onto a wire rack to cool.

8. Once your loaf is completely cool remove the paddle of your machine. For the very best results slice up your loaf with a serrated bread knife and serve while it is still warm.

26) French Style Bread Loaf

For bread fans, one of the most popular types of bread they purchase are French baguettes or French bread from their local supermarket. It probably never crossed your mind that you can make this bread right in the comfort of your own home. The only difference between homemade French bread and the kind that you can purchase you're a supermarket is that your homemade French bread will most likely be eaten in one day. This is the perfect bread to make for breakfast or as an item that you take along to a family picnic. Regardless, you are going to love this bread recipe.

Serving Size: 1 Loaf

Cooking Time: 50 Minutes

List of Ingredients:

- 1 ¼ Cups of Water, Warm
- 3 Cups of Bread Flour, White and Strong
- 1 ¼ teaspoons of Salt
- 1 ¼ teaspoons of Sugar
- 1 ½ teaspoons of Yeast, Fast Acting and Easy Blend Variety

sss

Methods:

1. Fix your mixing bowl securely to your bread maker before you add in any of the ingredients. Make sure that the paddle is also fixed in place securely. Leave your machine unplugged.

2. Add in your water and olive oil to your machine followed by half of bread flour.

3. Then add in your sugar, salt and your remaining flour.

4. Make a small well in the top of the flour and carefully place your yeast right into the center of it, making sure that it does not come into contact with any your liquid.

5. Close the lid of your machine and plug it into the wall. Set your machine to the French setting, which you can find in your machines manual. Feel free to alter the crust setting to your liking.

6. Once your bread is fully cooked carefully remove the bowl from your machine and remove the loaf. Place your loaf onto a wire rack to cool.

7. Once your loaf is completely cool remove the paddle of your machine. For the very best results slice up your loaf with a serrated bread knife and serve while it is still warm.

27) Chickpea and Peppercorn Colored Bread Loaf

The best thing about baking is that you can make virtually anything if you have all of the right ingredients. This loaf in particular is extremely colorful and you will be left with a loaf that is both light and extremely tasty. If you have trouble tracking down some colored peppercorns, don't hesitate to add some dried up mixed herbs instead.

Serving Size: 1 Loaf

Cooking Time: 1 Hour and 15 Minutes

List of Ingredients:

- 1 1/8 Cups of Water, Warm
- 2 Tablespoons Olive Oil, Light
- 1 Cup of Chickpeas, Tinned, Drained and Rinsed
- 3 2/5 Cups of Bread Flour, White and Strong
- 2 teaspoons of Pink Peppercorns, Drained and rinsed
- 2 teaspoons of Green Peppercorns, Drained and rinsed
- 1 ½ teaspoons of Salt

- 2 teaspoons of Sugar, White
- 1 ½ Tablespoons of Milk powder, Dried and Skimmed
- 1 ½ teaspoons of Yeast, Fast Acting and Easy Blend Variety

ssssssssssssssssssssssssssssssssssssssssssssssssssss

Methods:

1. Fix your mixing bowl securely to your bread maker before you add in any of the ingredients. Make sure that the paddle is also fixed in place securely. Leave your machine unplugged.

2. Add in your water, olive oil and chickpeas into your machine. Then add in half of your flour.

3. Then add in your colored peppercorns, salt, white sugar, milk powder and your remaining flour.

4. Make a small well in the top of the flour and carefully place your yeast right into the center of it, making sure that it does not come into contact with any your liquid.

5. Close the lid of your machine and plug it into the wall. Set your machine to the basic white bread loaf setting, which you can find in your machines manual. Feel free to alter the crust setting to your liking.

6. Once your bread is fully cooked carefully remove the bowl from your machine and remove the loaf. Place your loaf onto a wire rack to cool.

7. Once your loaf is completely cool remove the paddle of your machine. For the very best results slice up your loaf with a serrated bread knife and serve while it is still warm.

28) Tasty Yogurt and Bran Bread Loaf

I know that this bread loaf may sound like it would be far from appetizing, but it is exactly that. This bread loaf contains a ton of fiber and is ideal or those who want to get a daily dose of fiber. This is the perfect dish to make paired with some smoke salmon or easy salad lunch. The molasses that is used in this recipe adds a bit added taste to the loaf and will make a bread loaf that you will not want to put down.

Serving Size: 1 Loaf

Cooking Time: 1 Hour and 10 Minutes

List of Ingredients:

- 1 2/3 Cups of Bread Flour, White and Strong
- 1 2/5 Cups of Bread Flour, Whole meal, Brown and Strong
- ¾ Cup of Water, Warm
- ¾ Cup of Yogurt, Plain and Natural
- 1 ½ Tablespoons of Olive Oil, Light

- 2 Tablespoons of Molasses
- 1 ½ teaspoons of Salt
- 2/5 Cup of Wheat Bran
- 1 teaspoon of Yeast, Fast Acting and Easy Blend Variety

ssssssssssssssssssssssssssssssssssssssssssssssssss

Methods:

1. Fix your mixing bowl securely to your bread maker before you add in any of the ingredients. Make sure that the paddle is also fixed in place securely. Leave your machine unplugged.

2. Mix both of your flours together until they are well combined then add this to your machine along with your water, yogurt, molasses and olive oil.

3. Then add in your salt, wheat brand and your remaining flour.

4. Make a small well in the top of the flour and carefully place your yeast right into the center of it, making sure that it does not come into contact with any your liquid.

5. Close the lid of your machine and plug it into the wall. Set your machine to the white loaf setting, which you can find in your machines manual. Feel free to alter the crust setting to your liking.

6. Once your bread is fully cooked carefully remove the bowl from your machine and remove the loaf. Place your loaf onto a wire rack to cool.

7. Once your loaf is completely cool remove the paddle of your machine. For the very best results slice up your loaf with a serrated bread knife and serve while it is still warm.

29) Colorful Fruit Bread Loaf

This is yet another delicious fruit bread that I highly recommend trying for yourself. The sweet taste of the banana and dried mango will satisfy any sweet tooth that you may have. This bread is great with a bowl of fresh berries or a poached egg. Regardless you are going to love it.

Serving Size: 1 Loaf

Cooking Time: 1 Hour and 5 Minutes

List of Ingredients:

- ¼ Cups of Mango Juice or Tropical Juice, Fresh
- 7/8 Cup of Buttermilk
- 3 Tablespoons of Honey, The Best Quality
- 2 Bananas, Large in Size, Peeled and Smashed
- 3 2/5 Cups of Bread Flour, White and Strong
- 1 teaspoon of Salt
- 1 teaspoon of Yeast, Fast Acting and Easy Blend Variety
- 1/3 Cup of Mango, Dried and Chopped Finely

ssssssssssssssssssssssssssssssssssssssssssssssssssssss

Methods:

1. Fix your mixing bowl securely to your bread maker before you add in any of the ingredients. Make sure that the paddle is also fixed in place securely. Leave your machine unplugged.

2. Next add in your juice, honey and buttermilk into your machine.

3. Then add in your smashed banana, salt and your remaining flour.

4. Make a small well in the top of the flour and carefully place your yeast right into the center of it, making sure that it does not come into contact with any your liquid.

5. Close the lid of your machine and plug it into the wall. Set your machine to the basic white bread loaf setting, which you can find in your machines manual. Feel free to alter the crust setting to your liking.

6. Then add in your dried fruit to your machine next the moment that it completes its first kneading cycle.

7. Once your bread is fully cooked carefully remove the bowl from your machine and remove the loaf. Place your loaf onto a wire rack to cool.

8. Once your loaf is completely cool remove the paddle of your machine. For the very best results slice up your loaf with a serrated bread knife and serve while it is still warm.

30) Nutty Walnut and Buckwheat Bread Loaf

This is yet another recipe that use molasses and it makes the tastiest bread loaf that you will ever taste. The addition of the walnuts used in this recipe make the perfect loaf of bread and is one bread that you will want to serve during the holiday season.

Serving Size: 1 Loaf

Cooking Time: 1 Hour

List of Ingredients:

- 3 Cups of Bread Flour, White and Strong
- 3/5 Cup of Buckwheat Flour
- 1 3/8 Cups of Water, Warm
- 2 Tablespoons of Olive Oil or Walnut Oil, Light
- 1 tablespoon of Molasses
- 1 ½ teaspoons of Salt
- 1 teaspoon of Sugar
- 1 ½ Tablespoons of Milk Powder, Skimmed and Dried

- 1 teaspoon of Yeast, Fast Acting and Easy Blend Variety
- ¾ Cup of Walnuts, Finely Chopped

sssssssssssssssssssssssssssssssssssssssssssssssssssss

Methods:

1. Fix your mixing bowl securely to your bread maker before you add in any of the ingredients. Make sure that the paddle is also fixed in place securely. Leave your machine unplugged.

2. Mix both of your flours together until they are thoroughly combine and add this to your machine. Then add in your water, oil and molasses.

3. Then add in your salt, sugar, milk powder and your remaining flour.

4. Make a small well in the top of the flour and carefully place your yeast right into the center of it, making sure that it does not come into contact with any your liquid.

5. Close the lid of your machine and plug it into the wall. Set your machine to the basic white bread loaf setting, which you can find in your machines manual. Feel free to alter the crust setting to your liking.

6. Then add in your finely chopped walnuts to your machine next the moment that it completes its first kneading cycle.

7. Once your bread is fully cooked carefully remove the bowl from your machine and remove the loaf. Place your loaf onto a wire rack to cool.

8. Once your loaf is completely cool remove the paddle of your machine. For the very best results slice up your loaf with a serrated bread knife and serve while it is still warm.

31) Sweet Milk and Honey Bread Loaf

There is a recipe in this book that is very similar to this one, but rest assured this is recipe is much different. This recipe is much healthier as it is made with skimmed milk and one of the best quality of honey. This is the perfect recipe if you are looking for a comfort bread or want to be reminded of when your grandparents make bread. Serve this bread along with some fresh tea or coffee to yield the best results.

Serving Size: 1 Loaf

Cooking Time: 1 Hour

List of Ingredients:

- 1 ¼ Cup of Milk, Skimmed and At Room Temperature
- 3 Tablespoons of Honey, The Best Quality You Can Find
- 3 Cups of Bread Flour, White and Strong
- 2 Tablespoons of Butter, Soft
- 1 ½ teaspoons of Salt

- 1 ½ teaspoons of Yeast, Fast Acting and Easy Blend Variety

ssssssssssssssssssssssssssssssssssssssssssssssssssss

Methods:

1. Fix your mixing bowl securely to your bread maker before you add in any of the ingredients. Make sure that the paddle is also fixed in place securely. Leave your machine unplugged.

2. Then add in your quality honey and skimmed milk along with half of your flour.

3. Then add in your salt, softened butter and your remaining flour.

4. Make a small well in the top of the flour and carefully place your yeast right into the center of it, making sure that it does not come into contact with any your liquid.

5. Close the lid of your machine and plug it into the wall. Set your machine to the basic white bread loaf setting, which you can find in your machines manual. Feel free to alter the crust setting to your liking.

6. Once your bread is fully cooked carefully remove the bowl from your machine and remove the loaf. Place your loaf onto a wire rack to cool.

7. Once your loaf is completely cool remove the paddle of your machine. For the very best results slice up your loaf with a serrated bread knife and serve while it is still warm.

32) Early Morning Muesli Bread Loaf

If you are a fan of traditional toast every morning, you certainly have to try this recipe for yourself. This bread is perfect on its own or slathered with a healthy helping of butter. Feel free to try this bread with your morning coffee or with a dollop of your favorite yogurt spread out on the top of it. This bread is perfect for breakfast, lunch or dinner. I promise, you won't be able to get enough of it.

Serving Size: 1 Loaf

Cooking Time: 50 Minutes

List of Ingredients:

- 1 5/8 Cups of Water, Warm
- 2 Tablespoons of Olive Oil, Light
- 3 Cups of Bread Flour, Whole meal, Brown and Strong
- 1 ½ teaspoons of Salt
- 1 tablespoon of Brown Sugar, Soft and Light
- 2 Tablespoons of Milk Powder, Dried and Skimmed

- ½ Cup of Muesli
- 2 teaspoons of Yeast, Fast Acting and Easy Blend Variety

sssssssssssssssssssssssssssssssssssssssssssssssssssss

Methods:

1. Fix your mixing bowl securely to your bread maker before you add in any of the ingredients. Make sure that the paddle is also fixed in place securely. Leave your machine unplugged.

2. Next add in your warm water and olive oil to your machine. Follow up with adding half of your flour.

3. Then add in your salt, sugar, milk powder, muesli and your remaining flour.

4. Make a small well in the top of the flour and carefully place your yeast right into the center of it, making sure that it does not come into contact with any your liquid.

5. Close the lid of your machine and plug it into the wall. Set your machine to the whole meal or whole-wheat loaf setting, which you can find in your machines manual. Feel free to alter the crust setting to your liking.

6. Once your bread is fully cooked carefully remove the bowl from your machine and remove the loaf. Place your loaf onto a wire rack to cool.

7. Once your loaf is completely cool remove the paddle of your machine. For the very best results slice up your loaf with a serrated bread knife and serve while it is still warm.

33) Sweet Tasting Carrot Bread

While this loaf may sound as if it would be far from appetizing, I can promise you that you will love it. This bread is very colorful and is very tasty when you pair it with a filling and hearty stew or soup. This bread recipe tastes amazing regardless of the time of the year. This recipe is also dairy free, making it a tasty alternative for vegetarians or vegans.

Serving Size: 1 Loaf

Cooking Time: 1 Hour and 10 Minutes

List of Ingredients:

- 1 ½ Cups of Bread Flour, White and Strong
- 1 ½ Cups of Bread Flour, Whole meal, Brown and Strong
- 1 3/8 Cups of Carrot Juice, Fresh
- 2 Tablespoons of Olive Oil, Light
- 1 ¼ teaspoons of Salt
- 1 teaspoon of Sugar, White

- 1 ½ teaspoons of Nutmeg, Freshly Grated
- 1 ¼ teaspoons of Yeast, Fast Acting and Easy Blend Variety

sssssssssssssssssssssssssssssssssssssssssssssssssss

Methods:

1. Fix your mixing bowl securely to your bread maker before you add in any of the ingredients. Make sure that the paddle is also fixed in place securely. Leave your machine unplugged.

2. Mix both of your flours together until they are thoroughly combine and add this to your machine. Then add in your fresh carrot juice and light olive oil.

3. Then add in your salt, sugar, nutmeg and your remaining flour.

4. Make a small well in the top of the flour and carefully place your yeast right into the center of it, making sure that it does not come into contact with any your liquid.

5. Close the lid of your machine and plug it into the wall. Set your machine to the basic white bread loaf setting, which you can find in your machines manual. Feel free to alter the crust setting to your liking.

6. Once your bread is fully cooked carefully remove the bowl from your machine and remove the loaf. Place your loaf onto a wire rack to cool.

7. Once your loaf is completely cool remove the paddle of your machine. For the very best results slice up your loaf with a serrated bread knife and serve while it is still warm.

34) Sweet and Strong Cho coffee Bread

This bread is packed full of coffee and chocolate, making it one bread recipe that will satisfy the strongest of sweet teeth. This recipe is incredibly versatile so don't be afraid to get a little creative with it now and again. While it may take a bit of time to put together, trust me when I say that it is well worth it in the end.

Serving Size: 1 Loaf

Cooking Time: 1 Hour and 5 Minutes

List of Ingredients:

- 1 1/3 Cups of Bread Flour, White and Strong
- 1 1/3 Cups of Water, Warm
- 1 1/3 Cups of Flour, Whole Wheat
- 1 ½ Tablespoons of Vegetable Oil
- 1 ½ teaspoons of Salt
- 1/3 Cup of Cocoa Powder
- ½ Cup of Chocolate Chips, Semisweet

- 2 ¼ teaspoons of Yeast, Fast Acting and Easy Blend Variety
- 2 Envelopes of Mocha Cappuccino, Instant
- 3 Tablespoons of Milk Powder, Dry
- 3 Tablespoons of Honey, Raw

sssssssssssssssssssssssssssssssssssssssssssssssssssss

Methods:

1. Fix your mixing bowl securely to your bread maker before you add in any of the ingredients. Make sure that the paddle is also fixed in place securely. Leave your machine unplugged.

2. Mix both of your flours together until they are thoroughly combine and add this to your machine. Then add in your water, oil and half of your flour mixture.

3. Then add in your salt, milk powder, raw honey, instant cappuccino, vegetable oil, cocoa powder and your remaining flour into your bread machine next.

4. Make a small well in the top of the flour and carefully place your yeast right into the center of it, making sure that it does not come into contact with any your liquid.

5. Close the lid of your machine and plug it into the wall. Set your machine to the basic whole-wheat or multigrain loaf setting, which you can find in your machines manual. Feel free to alter the crust setting to your liking.

6. Then add in your finely semisweet chocolate chips to your machine next the moment that it completes its first kneading cycle.

7. Once your bread is fully cooked carefully remove the bowl from your machine and remove the loaf. Place your loaf onto a wire rack to cool.

8. Once your loaf is completely cool remove the paddle of your machine. For the very best results slice up your loaf with a serrated bread knife and serve while it is still warm.

Chapter II – Tasty Homemade Rolls

SSSSSSSSSSSSSSSSSSSSSSSSSSSSSSSSSSSSSSSSSSSSSSSSSSSS

35) Delicious Pita Bread

Pita bread is one of the most excellent appetizers that you can makes, especially when you serve with some herbed cream cheese or dip them in some freshly made hummus. You can even serve this with a course of meat and stuffed veggies or stuff the pita bread with some toppings like a sandwich. To top it all off this bread is relatively easy to make. With this recipe you will have enough pita bread that you can enjoy right now and store some for later use.

Serving Size: 2 Pita Breads

Cooking Time: 1 Hour and 10 Minutes

List of Ingredients:

- 2 Tablespoons of Yeast, Fast Acting and Easy Blend Variety
- 2 ½ Cups of Water, Warm
- 2 teaspoons of Salt
- 6 ½ Cups of Flour, All Purpose

ssssssssssssssssssssssssssssssssssssssssssssssssssss

Methods:

1. In your standing mixing, combine your yeast and warm water together and let it sit for at least 5 minutes or until your yeast has become frosty in consistency.

2. Next add in your salt and at least 3 cups of flour. Then using your dough hook attachment, beat your mixture together until it forms a thick batter. Then add the rest of your flour and continue to beat up your dough. Don't worry if it is rough or saggy at first. This is the way that it should be. Just continue mixing it for at least 8 minutes or until your dough is smooth and elastic in texture. If you notice that you dough is too sticky, add in a bit more flour, but only ¼ Cup at a time.

3. Spread your dough out on a lightly floured or oiled surface and separate your dough into 12 small balls. Roll each of these balls onto a thick circle and let them rest for at least 40 minutes or until they have risen slightly.

4. Next preheat your oven to 425 degrees. While your oven is heating up in line up a baking sheet with some parchment paper and turn your pitas upside down onto your baking sheet.

5. Place your baking sheet into your oven and let your pita bread bake for about 10 to 15 minutes or until they are lightly golden brown in color. Serve immediately and serve the rest. Enjoy.

36) Classic American Style Beer Bread

This type of bread is incredibly easy to make and will offer up a taste that even those who don't like beer will absolutely love. Since there is already yeast beer used in this recipe, you won't have to worry about using active yeast at all. The carbonation from the beer that you use will help the bread to rise to its desired consistency and it will taste both light and fluffy. Serve this bread alongside fresh jam and melted butter or serve with a tasty sandwich.

Serving Size: 1 Loaf

Cooking Time: 1 Hour and 30 Minutes

List of Ingredients:

- 12 Ounces of Light Beer, Blue Ribbon or Budweiser Preferable
- 3 Cups of Flour, Unbleached and All Purpose
- 1 ½ teaspoons of Sea Salt
- 1 tablespoon of Baking Powder
- ¼ Cup of Sugar, White

- 4 Tablespoons of Butter, Melted

ssssssssssssssssssssssssssssssssssssssssssssssssssssss

Methods:

1. The first thing that you will want to do is preheat your oven to 350 degrees. While your oven is heating up, prepare a baking sheet by spraying it with a generous amount of oil or coat it evenly with some flour.

2. Then using a large sized bowl, combine all of your dry ingredients together, whisking together with a wire whisk for at least 30 seconds to 1 minute.

3. Next add in your beer and carefully fold in your batter. Continue folding until all of the flour is blended in well, but make sure that you do not over mix it.

4. Pour your batter into a pan that is lightly floured and pour your melted butter over the top of it. Place this pan into your preheated oven and bake for about 55 minutes to 1 hour. Tent your loaf with some aluminum foil after it has finished baking for 40 minutes.

5. Once your loaf has finished baking, remove it from your oven and remove from your pan. Let it sit for about 15 minutes to cool slightly and slice it up.

37) Tasty Cheddar, Rosemary and Pancetta Biscuits

While this recipe may not be your traditional bread loaf recipe, it does not mean that it is not the least bit tasty. This recipe will give you a nice break from the typical dinner loaf and will give you biscuits that you are going to want to make again and again. These biscuits will pare greatly with any kind of Italian, American, French or Mediterranean meal that you cook up. Feel free to dip these biscuits in a savory soup or serve with just a touch of melted butter that will satisfy your entire family.

Serving Size: 12 Biscuits

Cooking Time: 1 Hour and 20 Minutes

List of Ingredients:

- 3 Cups of Flour, Unbleached and All Purpose
- 4 teaspoons of Baking Powder
- 1 teaspoon of Baking Soda
- ½ teaspoons of Sugar, White
- ½ teaspoons of Salt

- 1 ½ Sticks of Butter, Cold and Cut Into Small Cubes
- 2 Tablespoons of Rosemary, Fresh and Chopped Finely
- 4 Slices of Pancetta, Crispy and Chopped Finely
- 1 ½ Cups of Cheddar Cheese, Extra Sharp and Grated
- 1 ½ Cups of Milk, Whole

sssssssssssssssssssssssssssssssssssssssssssssssss

Methods:

1. The first thing that you will want to do is preheat your oven to 450 degrees. While your oven heats up line a baking sheet with some aluminum foil or parchment paper.

2. Fix your mixing bowl securely to your bread maker before you add in any of the ingredients. Make sure that the paddle is also fixed in place securely. Leave your machine unplugged.

3. Then add in your milk and half of your flour into your machine.

4. Next add in your salt, baking powder, baking soda, sugar, butter slices, rosemary, pancetta, cheddar cheese and your remaining flour into your bread machine next.

5. Close the lid of your machine and plug it into the wall. Set your machine to the basic white bread loaf setting, which you can find in your machines manual. Feel free to alter the crust setting to your liking.

6. Once your dough is sticky and lumpy in consistency, spoon your biscuits onto your baking sheet, making sure to form your biscuits into small circles that are about 3 to 4 inches in diameter. Also make sure that you leave about 2 inches in between each biscuit on your baking sheet. This is when you shouldn't worry about making the biscuits perfect. You will make mistakes from time to time.

7. Last, top your biscuits with some sharp cheddar cheese and sprinkle some fresh rosemary on top of it and then pop them into your oven for 13 and 15 minutes or until they are light brown around the edges and the top of the biscuits are bubbly. Serve and enjoy while they are still warm.

38) Tasty Dessert Style Maple and Bacon Cornbread

This is a creative twists on a traditional cornbread dish that you will want to add to virtually every meal that you prepare. This dish is incredibly versatile, so you can make it as one entire loaf or as individual muffins if you wish. I recommend serving this cornbread alongside a classic country style breakfast or dinner. You will love it regardless of when you serve it.

Serving Size: 1 Loaf Cornbread

Cooking Time: 40 Minutes

List of Ingredients:

- 1 Cup of Flour, Unbleached and All Purpose
- 1 Cup of Cornmeal
- ½ teaspoons of Salt
- 1 tablespoon of Baking Powder
- 3 to 4 Slices of Bacon, Fully Cooked, Crispy and Diced Finely
- ¼ Cup of Maple Syrup, Room Temperature

- 1 Cup of Milk, Warm
- 2 Tablespoons of Butter, Melted
- 2 Tablespoons of Bacon Grease
- 2 Eggs, Large in Size and At Room Temperature

sssssssssssssssssssssssssssssssssssssssssssssssssssss

Methods:

1. The first thing that you will want to do is preheat your oven to 425 degrees. Then using a large sized bowl or the bowl of your standing mixer, mix together all of your dry ingredients together until thoroughly combined.

2. Then using a separate medium sized mixing bowl mix together your milk, syrup, bacon grease, eggs, butter and diced up bacon pieces together until evenly mixed.

3. Next add your wet ingredients to your dry ingredients until mixed. Do this for at least 5 minutes to ensure even mixing.

4. Pour your newly created batter into a greased up baking pan. Place your pan into your oven to bake for at least 20 to 25 minutes or until golden brown in color. Serve this while still warm and drizzled with some maple syrup and butter and enjoy immediately.

39) Gold Pretzel Rolls

These rolls are one of the best type of rolls to make and it will soon become your favorite type of roll. These are great rolls to serve alongside a delicious gourmet sandwich such as Tuscany Chicken Sandwich or classic Reuben sandwich. Or you can easily serve these rolls with a gourmet dinner and some melted butter. Either way it will be delicious and you will want to make it over and over again.

Serving Size: 16 Rolls

Cooking Time: 1 Hour and 30 Minutes

Ingredients for Your Dough:

- 1 ¼ Cup of Milk, Warm
- ½ Cup of Water, Warm
- ½ teaspoons of Salt
- 1 ½ Tablespoons of Vegetable Oil
- 1 tablespoon of Sugar, White
- 1 tablespoon of Yeast, Fast Acting and Easy Blend Variety
- 3 to 4 Cups of Flour, Unbleached and All Purpose
- Dash of Kosher Salt or Sea Salt

Ingredients for Your Wash:

- 5 Cups of Water, Warm
- 1 tablespoon of Salt
- 4 Tablespoons of Baking Soda

sssssssssssssssssssssssssssssssssssssssssssssssssss

Methods:

1. The first thing that you will want to do is preheat your oven to 450 degrees. While your oven heats up line a baking sheet with some aluminum foil or parchment paper.

2. Fix your mixing bowl securely to your bread maker before you add in any of the ingredients. Make sure that the paddle is also fixed in place securely. Leave your machine unplugged.

3. Then add in your milk and half of your flour into your machine.

4. Next add in your salt, sugar, yeast, water and vegetable oil and your remaining flour into your bread machine next.

5. Mix up your dough for a couple of minutes until you have the perfect round of dough on your hands. Remove from your machine and knead your dough for about 2 to 3 minutes or until no more air bubbles form.

6. Then move your dough to a warm place and cover with a bit of plastic wrap. Let your dough rise for the next 50 to 60 minutes or until the dough itself has doubled in size. Once your dough has risen punch it down and knead the dough on an oiled surface to bring it all back together.

7. Once your dough is sticky and lumpy in consistency, tear your biscuits onto your baking sheet, making sure to form your biscuits into small circles that are about 3 to 4 inches in diameter. Also make sure that you leave about 2 inches in between each biscuit on your baking sheet. This is when you shouldn't worry about making the biscuits perfect. You will make mistakes from time to time.

8. Prepare your dough wash next by combining all of your ingredients together. The moment your dough balls have sat for 15 minutes, dip them into your wash and place them back onto your baking sheet.

9. Place your rolls into your oven to bake for 20 to 15 minutes or until they are deep brown in color. Serve the moment you take them out of the oven. Enjoy!

40) American Style Indian Fry-bread

This is a type of flat bread that usually makes an appearance at state fairs as one of the tastiest desserts that you have ever tasted. However, this is one dish that can be prepared for dinner as well. I recommend making this bread as a shell for tacos topped with beans, cheese, sour cream and mild pico de gallo. These frybreads are delicious when drizzled over with honey while they are still warm to the touch.

Serving Size: 4 Frybreads

Cooking Time: 45 Minutes

List of Ingredients:

- 6 Cups of Flour, All Purpose
- 3 teaspoons of Salt
- 3 teaspoons of Baking Powder
- ½ Cup of Sugar, Granulated and White
- 2 ½ Cups of Water, Warm
- 1 Cup of Vegetable Oil

sssssssssssssssssssssssssssssssssssssssssssssssssssssssss

Methods:

1. Using a large sized bowl or a bowl in your standing mixer, combine all of your dry ingredients together until they are well combined. Then add in your warm water and mix together on the lowest or medium speed setting while using your dough hook until the dough is well combined and it is elastic in consistency. Keep in mind that your dough will still be somewhat moist but it will not be too sticky. If you have to add a little bit of flour or water if your dough is too dry or too wet.

2. Add some flour or oil onto a flat surface and tear your dough into large sized balls of dough. Roll out each ball of dough until they are circular in shape and about ¼ inch thick. Keep in mind that the dough will still be very elastic so make sure to roll it out gently until they are the perfect size and proper thickness.

3. Then using a large sized frying pan, preheat your vegetable oil over medium to high heat. Then using a pair of cooking tongs place each piece of your frypan into your oil and let it fry until both sides are light gold in color. Remove and set on a few paper towels to drain and allow to cool for about 3 to 5 minutes before serving.

41) Classic Italian Garlic Knots

If you have ever tried classic garlic knots at an Italian restaurant, you are going to love this recipe. These garlic knots go great when paired with some pasta, fresh salad and a glass of wine. Prepare this recipe as an appetizer and dip them in some freshly prepared marinara sauce or garlic butter sauce.

Serving Size: 16 Garlic Knots

Cooking Time: 1 Hour and 45 Minutes

Ingredients for Your Dough:

- 1 ¾ Cups of Water, Warm
- ¼ Cup of Olive Oil, Extra Virgin
- 1 ½ teaspoons of Sea Salt
- 1 ½ Tablespoons of Sugar, White
- 1 ½ Tablespoons of Yeast, Fast Acting and Easy Blend Variety
- 5 to 6 Cups of Flour, Unbleached or All Purpose

Ingredients for Your Garlic and Cheese Toppings:

- ¼ Cup of Butter, Softened
- ¼ Cup of Olive Oil, Extra Virgin
- 5 Cloves of Garlic, Minced or Crushed
- 3 Tablespoons of Italian Parsley, Fresh and Finely Chopped
- ¼ Cup of Romano Cheese, Grated
- ¼ Cup of Parmesan Cheese, Grated
- 1 teaspoon of Sea Salt

ssssssssssssssssssssssssssssssssssssssssssssssssssssssss

Methods:

1. The first thing that you will want to do is preheat your oven to 400 degrees. While your oven heats up line a baking sheet with some aluminum foil or parchment paper.

2. Using a large sized mixing combine your water, sugar, salt and yeast together until the yeast has fully dissolved. Then add in 5 cups of your flour and mix until it is evenly combined. Keep adding flour in little by little or until the dough is no longer sticky.

3. Once your dough is ready knead it by hand or with your bread machine until it is thoroughly worked through. Cover your dough with some plastic wrap and place it into your refrigerator for at least 1 hour.

4. After an hour remove your dough and slice it up into small balls of dough. Once your dough is sticky and lumpy in consistency, tear your balls of dough onto your baking sheet, making sure to form your biscuits into small circles that are about 3 to 4 inches in diameter. Carefully knot up your dough into simple knots. Also make sure that you leave about 2 inches in between each knot on your baking sheet. This is when you shouldn't worry about making the knots perfect. You will make mistakes from time to time.

5. Cover your knots with plastic wrap and allow them to rise for an additional 30 minutes to an hour or until they have doubled in size.

6. Place your knots into your oven to bake for 12 to 15 minutes or until they are golden brown in color.

7. While your knots are baking combine your butter, olive oil, garlic and sea salt together over medium heat in a medium sized saucepan. Cook your ingredients until the butter has melted completely. Then in a separate bowl mix together your grated cheeses and Italian parsley. Mix until they are thoroughly combined.

8. Once your knots are done baking remove them from your oven and brush them with your butter mixture and toss into your cheese mixture. Serve your rolls immediately and enjoy.

About the Author

Allie Allen developed her passion for the culinary arts at the tender age of five when she would help her mother cook for their large family of 8. Even back then, her family knew this would be more than a hobby for the young Allie and when she graduated from high school, she applied to cooking school in London. It had always been a dream of the young chef to study with some of Europe's best and she made it happen by attending the Chef Academy of London.

After graduation, Allie decided to bring her skills back to North America and open up her own restaurant. After 10 successful years as head chef and owner, she decided to sell her business and pursue other career avenues. This monumental decision led Allie to her true calling, teaching. She also started to write e-books for her students to study at home for practice. She is now the proud author of several e-books and gives private and semi-private cooking lessons to a range of students at all levels of experience.

Stay tuned for more from this dynamic chef and teacher when she releases more informative e-books on cooking and baking in the near future. Her work is infused with stores and anecdotes you will love!

Author's Afterthoughts

I can't tell you how grateful I am that you decided to read my book. My most heartfelt thanks that you took time out of your life to choose my work and I hope you find benefit within these pages.

There are so many books available today that offer similar content so that makes it even more humbling that you decided to buying mine.

Tell me what you thought! I am eager to hear your opinion and ideas on what you read as are others who are looking for a good book to buy. Leave a review on Amazon.com so others can benefit from your wisdom!

With much thanks,

Allie Allen

Printed in Great Britain
by Amazon

39289696R00083